A COUNTRY
KITCHEN

...bringing 1:24th to life

GW00683486

Fiona Broadwood

2007

A **LUMO PUBLISHING** BOOK

First published in the UK in 2007

Design Copyright © Fiona Broadwood 2007

Photography and Layout Copyright © Fiona Broadwood 2007

A catalogue record for this book is available from the British Library

ISBN 978-0-9555344-0-9

Photography by Fiona Broadwood & Chloe (Mo) Broadwood

Book Design by Fiona Broadwood & Lucy Broadwood

Printed by Norton Print for **LUMO PUBLISHING**.

The projects in this book **are not** suitable for children.

For my husband Tony.

My guardian.
From beginning to end...

contents...

foreword...

Dear Reader

As a dolls house builder I have always preferred to work in the 1:24th scale, as I have found architectural details can be accurately achieved without difficulty.

Contrary to popular belief, it is incredibly easy to create and build in this smaller scale, with furniture and room features being no exception. Houses, cottages or shops can be filled with handmade furniture and accessories at very little cost.

In my (humble) opinion 1:24 is becoming the ultimate D.I.Y scale and as such it is easy to see why it is rapidly growing in popularity.

Lack of space? No problem!

If space is at a premium then the 1:24th scale is definitely for you. Half scale doll's houses take up very little space, when compared to their larger 1:12th counterparts. The smaller size also allows miniaturists to collect many individual houses, instead of just one or two. Street scenes can be recreated and displayed in the space of a simple wall shelf.

If, as an avid miniaturist, you are reluctant to restrict your dolls house ownership to just one architectural period or style of property, then the smaller scale houses are for you... **as less, can mean more!**

1:24th scale collectors can display, many different houses, cottages or shops in the same space that is needed to accommodate just <u>one</u> 12th scale dolls house.

As a result of my work I am constantly asked by my customers where they can find realistic furniture and accessories for their new cottages and also, how best to decorate their 24th scale interiors in order to bring them to life?

Quite simply, from now on... this book will be my reply.

Fiona Broadwood
(Bea)

welcome to 1:24th scale...

For all readers new to this scale and for those who maybe embarking on their very first 1:24th scale project, I feel that I should begin by clarifying the *'science bit'* of working in this wonderful smaller scale.

The ratio or scale - **1:24** translates simply into:

1 foot = ½ an inch

So for example, a measurement of 1 inch x 2 inches given for a 1:24th scale table top, would translate into a 2 foot x 4 foot table top if it were to be made in real life.

It is also worth noting that the 1:24th scale is sometimes referred to as **half inch scale** or **half scale**, as when compared to the larger and more common 1:12th scale, (1 foot = 1 inch) it is quite simply – **half the size.**

Please note: The measurements in the project methods within this book are all given in inches, where the abbreviation 'in' = inch is used.

"the aims of this book..."

This book has been written to inspire owners of 1:24th scale dolls houses to create an imaginative country kitchen, filled with realistic furniture and traditional features. With the aid of step-by-step instructions, combined with easy to understand diagrams and pictures, 1:24th scale kitchen interiors can be transformed and brought to life with minimal expense.

Alternatively the country kitchen featured in this book, can be made as an individual room box, an ideal introduction for anyone new to the 1:24th scale.

"No woodwork required..."

Each project in this book has been designed for "mini-makers" of all levels of ability and uniquely **does not** feature the use of hard wood, nor will you require any complicated wood working skills to complete them. Instead, basic art and craft materials are combined with the clever adaptation of every day objects to produce a wide range of kitchen furniture and room features.

tools...

When I developed the projects for this book, my main aim was to keep the tools required as simple as possible, you will probably have most of them already.

Many of the 'makes' feature the same tools and materials, just simply utilised in different ways.

Stanley knife or Craft knife: Use whichever knife you feel more comfortable with. I use a combination of the two. For example when I cut mount board which is quite thick, I use a Stanley Knife and for thinner card and more intricate work I use a craft knife.

Metal Ruler: After painful mistakes, I strongly recommend you use one with a finger guard and for added safety and accuracy, one with a non slip backing helps to keep the ruler in position whilst cutting.

Pencil: It might sound obvious, but make sure your pencil is well sharpened, as a fine point helps keep measurements precise and accurate.

Bristle brushes: I have always used a widely available children's range of chunky brushes as they are both effective and very economical to use.

Fine paint brushes: I recommend a 'general' selection of water colour brushes. They allow a good quality of finish and are ideal for painting many of the projects in this book.

Garden secateurs: I have found these to be the most easy and effective way to cut matchsticks.

Scissors: Small and large craft scissors. Curved nail scissors are also helpful when cutting out rounded shapes.

Elastic bands: Various sizes for holding parts in place when gluing.

Clothes pegs: Are useful to hold glued card together if like me, you run out of hands!

Tweezers: These are ideal for handling and positioning small items such as furniture handles.

Set square: For accurate marking of 90° and 45° angles.

Hole punch: Any good quality office variety will do.

Kitchen sponge: Firm and dense sponges are best. They can be cut to the required size.

Cotton buds: To remove and clean away excess glue etc.

Cutting board: A4 size is ideal.

Wire cutters: The smaller, the better.

materials...

The following list is an overview of the basic materials required to complete the projects in this book.

Further information is supplied for any special material requirements for individual projects at the beginning of each set of project instructions.

All materials required are readily available from any good art or craft shop, high street stationary store or even well stocked market stalls.

- Mount card
- Foam board (or similar)*
- Medium card - cereal boxes are ideal for some projects.
- Black paper
- Beads - selection of styles and sizes
- Balsa wood - 'off cuts' are sufficient.
- Paint - including emulsion, poster paint and acrylic varieties.
- Varnish - matt finish & high gloss finish
- Matchsticks

- Garden wire
- Soft tissues
- Large and regular sized metal paperclips.
- Adhesives - PVA, tacky glue and double sided sticky tape
- A clear plastic margarine or butter tub lid* (or similar)- with which to glaze the two small windows.
- Buttons - see page 12
- Masking tape
- Dress making pins
- x 2 plastic 1:24th scale windows*

*only required if you wish to make the actual kitchen room box itself
- See page 38 for further details...

paint...

Paint... Now there's a subject!

In my opinion paint is a very personal thing. Some people like to use acrylics, whilst others are happy to dab on poster paint. Colours are also an individual choice, influenced by personal preference and by the type of project or period of house you are working on. With this in mind I have given examples below of the types of paint that can be used and also the colours that I personally prefer, highlighted in italics. Remember, there are no right or wrong choices, instead simply what works for you.

Poster Paint...

I have used this type of paint in my 'mortar paint' mix and also for the flagstone floor on page 40. Poster paints are both cheap and versatile and are also excellent when mixed with matt emulsion to create any desired tone or colour. They also help to make more expensive paints, go that little bit further. *(Black, yellow, brown)*

Emulsion tester pots...

These are really useful and come in an infinite range of colours. Most 'tester pots' are only available in a matt finish, which can be easily sealed, if required with a single coat of either matt, satin or gloss finish varnish. I particularly like and use the period inspired colour ranges. Although they are initially more expensive to purchase, they contain a much higher level of pigment and in turn will provide excellent coverage. It may also be helpful to note that some period inspired paint ranges offer additional information on their colour charts. This historical information is helpful if you want to be able to select individual colours to recreate and reflect specific period styles or architectural influences. *(Off white, ivory and cream)*

Acrylic paints...

I use this paint a lot and have found that it can easily be mixed to create desired shades and tones as required. There are many inexpensive ranges available, offering an extremely wide selection of colours.

(Pale biscuit, medium brown, dark brown etc.)

Satin wood / Egg shell...

I would only recommend this type of paint for painting furniture. It is ideal if you don't want to have to seal your work with varnish after it has been painted. I would also only advise the use of the water based paints in these finishes, as I have found that they not only dry quickly, but also brushes can be easily cleaned with hot soapy water after use. [Cream and ivory.]

Varnish...

Technically not a 'paint' I know, but as I have previously mentioned varnish can be used to seal a variety of matt finish paints. I would advise using a water based varnish as they are normally quick drying, easy to use and give excellent even results. Ranges of water based varnishes normally include matt, satin and high gloss finishes.

"Homemade paint mixes..."

'Mucky' paint mix...

This homemade paint mix is used to distress the rough render on the walls and chimney breast in the farmhouse kitchen. Simply mix together a little brown, yellow and black poster paint then dilute with water until the mixture resembles muddy puddle water. As with all homemade paint mixes the colour is not an exact science, simply whatever shade and colour of 'dirtiness' that works for you. Excess paint can be stored in jam jars, but remember to shake well and stir thoroughly before use.

'Beam' paint mix...

This is a simple water based mix of poster paint. Blend a little medium brown and black poster paint together, then dilute with enough water to make the final paint mix into a translucent solution that will gently '*stain*' the wooden beams, rather than 'paint' them.

'Mortar' paint mix...

This paint mix is not meant to be as watery as the two previous homemade mixes and should be of a normal paint consistency. The colour to aim for, for the pot sink mortar mix is a 'muddy green'. Take some yellow poster paint and add a little black poster paint. Blend in a little blue to create the green tint. Mix well and store excess paint in a jam jar.

For the flagstone floor add more yellow paint and less blue to the mix in order to get a 'sandy' mortar colour for painting between the flagstone slabs.

paint techniques...

The paint techniques used in this book are not complicated to master and there isn't a long list of difficult skills which need to be learnt and perfected. With the exception of good old fashioned painting there are really only two techniques to get to grips with and both are as simple as each other - trust me!

"Dry brush distressing..."

All of the projects in this book involve a certain amount of 'dirtying' in order to give them an 'aged and used' appearance and it is this that makes the finished piece look so effective. 'Dry brush distressing' is the best technique that I have developed for this purpose and simply involves a tiny amount of paint, applied in gentle circular movements, with a completely dry brush. Paint then catches onto the edges of details such as drawers and doors and gives a softer, lived in look to furniture and features. Applying the 'dry brush technique over matt paint will give a dirtier finish as the matt paint will absorb more of the distressing colour used.

"Sponging..."

I am sure that most of you will already be familiar with this very common painting technique. I have found that a gentle dabbing motion, combined with a relatively small amount of paint, spread over a dry firm sponge, gives the best results. This technique is ideal for creating the realistic flagstone floor project on page 41 and helps to bring the pot sink's bricks to life on page 23.

"Room features..."

the fireplace...

Materials...

- Mount board
- x2 lengths of balsa wood: *see fig. 3 for measurements*
- Tissues
- Matt emulsion: tester pot in chosen room colour
- 'Mucky' paint mix: *see pg. 6*
- 'Beam' paint mix: *see pg. 6*
- Black poster paint
- Paper tile 'cut-outs': *see pg.46*
- Grain of wheat light
- Balsa wood 'off cut' for mantle beam
- x2 wooden toothpicks
- PVA adhesive
- Tacky glue

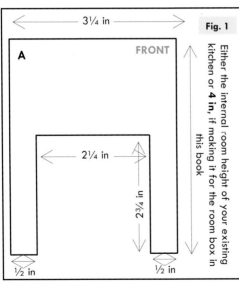

Fig. 1

A — FRONT

3¼ in

2¼ in

2¾ in

½ in   ½ in

Either the internal room height of your existing kitchen or **4 in**, if making it for the room box in this book

Fig. 2

¾ in   B   FALSE CEILING

2¼ in

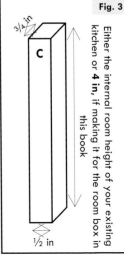

Fig. 3

¾ in   C   ½ in

Either the internal room height of your existing kitchen or **4 in**, if making it for the room box in this book

Step 1...

Draw out fireplace front: **part A** (see fig. 1) and **part B** (see fig. 2) onto mount board. Cut out using a craft knife and metal rule.

9

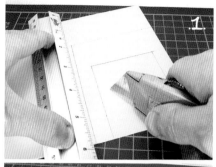

Step 2...

Cut x2 pieces of balsa wood to measurements given in *fig. 3* and glue onto the rear of **part A**, see picture 2.

Step 3...

Make a small hole in the centre of **part B** large enough to thread the bulb of a grain of wheat light through. Paint one side with two coats of black poster paint. When dry, glue into place half way between the top of the chimney breast and the fireplace aperture. (see *fig. 4* on pg. 11) and with the black side facing downwards.

Step 4...

Liberally coat the exterior of the fireplace in PVA adhesive, then cover with shredded pieces of tissue sheets. Allow the tissue to wrinkle up and crease, as this will add texture to the final wall finish. Patch any areas not covered using small torn sections of tissue. Allow to dry completely, ideally leave over night.

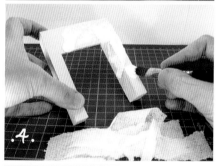

Step 5...

Paint the rough rendered fireplace with two coats of matt emulsion. I have used an ivory colour, but any off white, or cream shade would be suitable. Leave to dry completely before continuing to step 6.

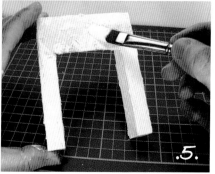

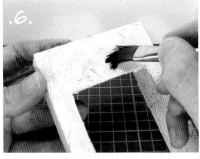

Step 6...

Distress the fireplace using the **dry brush technique:** Take a completely dry, clean brush and load with a small amount of the mucky paint mix. With a dry piece of kitchen paper remove the excess paint from the brush until the bristles are almost dry again. Apply the paint with gentle circular movements, working lightly over the entire fireplace. The mucky paint will 'catch' upon the rough surface and age the uneven render.

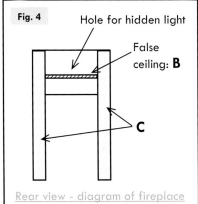

Fig. 4

Hole for hidden light

False ceiling: **B**

C

Rear view - diagram of fireplace

Step 7...

Thread the bulb of a grain of wheat light

through the hole previously made in **part B**, see picture 7. Make an additional hole in the wall of the room box, behind the final location of the fireplace. Take the wire through this hole and electrify as per the manufacturer's instructions. Cut out the paper tiles for the kitchen fireplace, see page 46, and glue onto the rear of the fireplace. Glue the fireplace into it's permanent position and cover up the joins between the fireplace, walls and ceiling with extra tissue layers. Touch up with paint and distress accordingly.

Step 8...

Take an 'off cut' of balsa wood and using a craft knife, round the edges. Add notches and cuts to age the wood's appearance, see picture 8a. Paint with the 'beam paint' solution on pg. 6. Allow to dry. Distress with a tiny amount of black poster paint, using the dry brush technique. Paint and distress 2 toothpicks in the same way as the mantle beam. Make 3 pilot holes into the beam using the sharp end of a toothpick. Cut off 3 toothpick tips and push them through the beam, from the back to the front to create pegs. Glue mantle beam onto fireplace. See picture 8b

a country range...

Materials...

- Mount card & Medium card
- Black paper (hole punched)
- Cream acrylic paint or tester pot of cream emulsion in desired colour.
- Gloss varnish - if a gloss finish is required
- Black & dark brown acrylic paint
- Bendable plastic straw
- x1 10mm metal washer
- x2 black buttons: ⅝in diameter
- Garden wire
- Tacky glue
- Large metal paper clip

Step 1...

Draw out the shapes shown in *Fig. 5* onto mount board and label each piece in pencil. Cut out each shape using a craft knife and metal ruler.

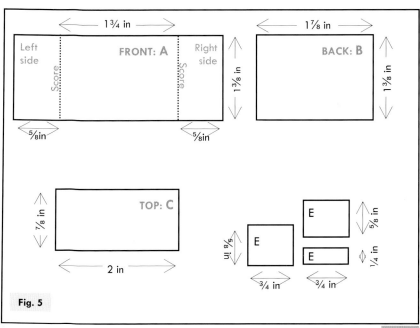

Fig. 5

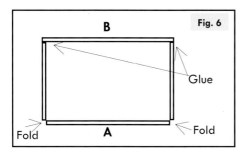

Fig. 6

B

Glue

Fold   A   Fold

Step 2...

Take front, **part A** and score deeply along the two dotted lines as shown in *fig. 5* Fold back the left and right sides and glue on **part B**. See *fig. 6 and picture 2*. Hold in place with an elastic band until dry.

Step 3...

Glue along the top edge of the range and position **part C** onto the top. Clean off any excess glue with a cotton bud.

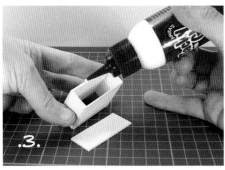

Step 4...

Cut a strip of medium card approximately 4in long x ¼in wide and glue along the bottom edge of the range, see picture 4. Continue to wrap the card strip around both sides to form a continuous plinth at the base of the range.

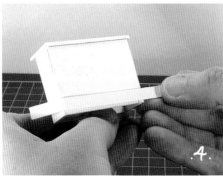

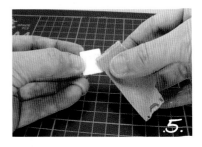

Step 5...

Snip off the sharp corner tips of all 3 door fronts; **parts E**, then using fine sand paper, sand the edges of all of the doors until they are gently rounded.

Glue into position on the front of the range, see picture 6 on page 14.

Step 6...

Cut 7 tiny lengths of garden wire. Bend one end of each piece of wire into a gentle curve. Glue into place onto the door fronts to form hinges and handles, with the curved ends of the wire bending over the rounded edges of the doors. Cut a tiny rectangle of medium card and position above the main oven door to form a simple maker's badge. Leave to dry.

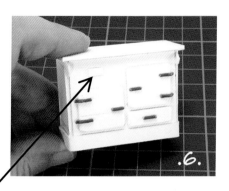

Step 7...

Take 2 pieces of hole punched card. Cut each circle in half and glue each half together to form two card semi circles.

Glue into the top edge of the scored card groove on the front of the range, on each side, see picture 7.

Leave to dry.

Step 8...

Paint range with 2 coats of acrylic or emulsion paint in your desired colour scheme. For the range pictured in this project I have used a deep cream paint. Once the range is completely dry apply 2 coats of black acrylic paint to the top and base plinth. Leave to dry.

Step 9...

Using the dry brush technique, distress the range with a tiny amount of dark brown acrylic paint, gently working over all of the cream areas. Leave to dry. Finish with 2 coats of quick dry gloss varnish if a shiny finish is desired.

14

Step 10...

Take two black buttons approximately ⅝in, in diameter and glue upside down into position on top of the range to form 'hot plate lids'. Next cut or hole punch 2 circles from black paper; large enough to cover the stitching holes on the buttons and glue in place. Finish off with two small cylindrical black beads glued onto the front of each button to create the appearance of handles, see picture 10.

.10.

Step 11...

For the front hand rail, unwind a large metal paperclip. Measure between the two semi circle card supports *(made in step 7)* and cut the paper clip to length with wire cutters. Glue in place in between the 2 semi circular brackets to form a hand rail.

.12b.

.12a.

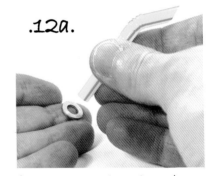

Step 12...

To create the flu, cut a bendy plastic straw to desired height and length. Cut the top of the flu at an appropriate angle that will allow the end of the flu to sit flush against the tiles when the range is in position in the fireplace. Glue the washer to the base of the flu, see picture 12a and once fully dry, paint with 2 coats of acrylic black paint. Glue the flu into place, onto the top of the range, see picture 12b, once the range is permanently positioned within the kitchen fireplace.

This range cooker has been designed to fit into the kitchen fireplace project on page 9. The range can be painted in any colour to suit any colour scheme and can also be widened if a larger cooker is required.

the pantry...

Materials...

- Mount board & tissues
- Balsa wood off cut: *2in long x 1in wide x ½in depth*
- Balsa wood beam: *length = Room height x ¼in width x ¼in depth*
- PVA adhesive & tacky glue
- Mucky paint mix, see pg. 6
- Emulsion: tester pot in chosen room colour
- Dark brown acrylic paint
- Black poster paint
- x5 small beads
- Medium card off cuts

Top tip...

When the pantry is finished it is easier to fill it and dress it with food <u>before</u> it is permanently fixed into position in the kitchen.

Step 1...

Draw out the shapes shown in *fig. 7* onto mount board. Label each piece in pencil with the corresponding letter as shown below to avoid mistakes during construction. Cut out each shape using a craft knife and metal ruler. **Do not** cut out the door shape, just mark the door out in pencil then proceed to step 2...

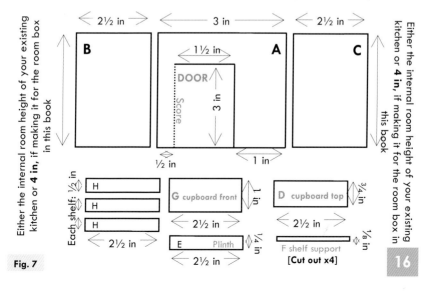

Fig. 7

Step 2...

Take **part A** and score along the dotted line (**do not** cut all the way through the card!) Next cut out the right side and top of the door shape marked onto the card. Trim the top, right side and bottom of the door (*See picture 2*) as this will allow the door to open and close more easily.

.3.

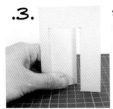

Step 3...

Gently fold the door inwards along the scored line, see picture 3.

Step 4...

Cut irregular strips of medium card. Cut 2 lengths to fit the width of the door and fit one to both the top and bottom. Measure the strips to fit vertically in between. Allow the glue to dry.

Step 5...

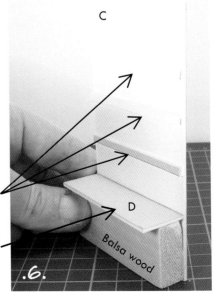

Paint the door with 2 coats of brown acrylic paint. Set aside to dry.

Step 6...

Take a piece of balsa wood: *2ins long x 1in wide x ½in deep* and glue to the bottom of **part C**. Next glue on the 3 shelf support strips: **parts F**, spacing them equally, *see picture 6*.

Glue **part D** onto the top of the balsa wood to form the top of the base cupboard within the pantry. Allow to dry.

.7 and 8.

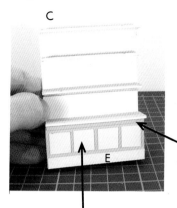

C

E

Step 7...

Take **part G** and glue it onto the front of the balsa wood to form the front of the base cupboard. Next glue the 3 shelves: **parts H** into place. Clean away any excess glue with a cotton bud. Glue the plinth: **part E** into place at the bottom of the base cupboard.

Finally, glue the 4th shelf support: **part F** to the top of the cupboard front, fitting it neatly under the cupboard top over hang. Allow to dry.

Step 8...

Mark and cut out 4 cupboard doors: ½in x ½in from an off cut of medium card. Glue into position onto the front of the base cupboard, spacing equally. Allow to dry.

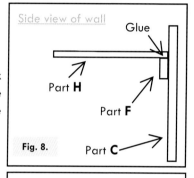

Side view of wall

Glue

Part **H**

Part **F**

Fig. 8.

Part **C**

Step 9...

Paint with 2 coats of brown acrylic paint. Allow to dry completely before distressing. Using the dry brush technique, distress the shelves with a tiny amount of cream emulsion to give a 'worn out' look. Finish by gluing 4 small beads onto the door front as handles.

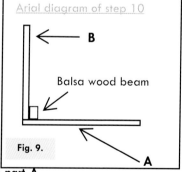

Arial diagram of step 10

B

Balsa wood beam

Fig. 9.

A

C

.9.

Step 10...

Glue **part B** to **part A**, see *fig. 9*. Next take a length of balsa wood and glue it into the corner to keep both panty walls at right angles to each other. Leave to dry completely.

.10.

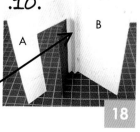

A

B

Step 11...

Once the front and left pantry walls are fully dry and the structure has strengthened, use some black poster paint and distress the pantry door with the *dry brush technique*. Once dry, glue on a small bead as a door handle on the outside of the pantry's door.

Step 12...

Cover the outside pantry walls with PVA glue. then cover with shredded pieces of tissue sheets. Allow the tissue to wrinkle up and crease as this will add texture to the final wall finish. Patch any areas not covered using small torn sections of tissue. Allow to dry completely, ideally leave over night. When the render is dry do not become concerned if the mount board has bent out of shape, particularly to the left of the door, as the board can easily and gently be bent back into place. Repeat the tissue render process on the inside wall of the pantry. Once again leave to completely dry out and until the structure is rigid.

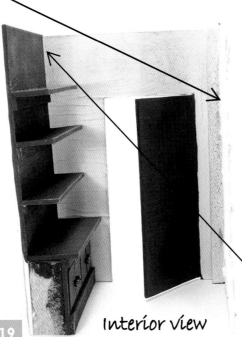

Interior view

Step 13...

Paint and distress the rendered walls in the same way as the exterior of the fireplace: see steps 5 and 6 on pages 10 and 11.

Step 14...

The interior shelves: **part C** can be fitted directly to the wall of your kitchen, with the left hand part of the pantry slotted in, to butt up to both the right and rear walls.

The pantry can be easily lit, by concealing a grain of wheat bulb behind the pantry door.

pot sink on bricks...

Materials...

- Air hardening clay
- x3 pieces of balsa wood
  (Please see figs 10 and 11 for measurements...)
- Mount card
- Tester pot of emulsion paint in a brick / terracotta colour
- Mortar paint mix: see pg. 6
- Brown, black & pale biscuit coloured acrylic paint
- Tester pot of 'off white' emulsion or eggshell finish paint
- Paper tile 'cut-outs': see pg. 46
- Small length of garden wire
- x1 small bead
- Tacky glue & fine sandpaper

Step 1...

Cut **1** length of balsa wood as shown in *fig. 10.* and **x2** lengths of balsa wood as shown in *fig. 11.* Using fine sand paper, sand the ends of all 3 pieces until smooth.

Steps 2 and 3...

Take a small piece of air hardening clay and roll out into a thin strip. Cover the balsa wood with tacky glue on all 4 sides, but not the ends. Wrap the clay around the wood, *(see picture 2)* making sure that the join is on one of the short sides of the balsa wood. Press the clay firmly against the wooden block and ensure that the clay's thickness is even. Trim the ends, *see picture 3 below.*

Fig. 10

A

1 1/4 in

1/4 in   3/4 in

Fig. 11

B

3/4 in

1/4 in   3/4 in

.2.

.3.

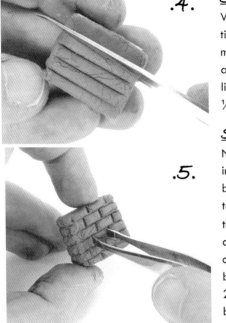

.4.

.5.

Step 4...

Working quickly on one block at a time, use a thin knife edge to carefully mark horizontal lines into the clay on all 4 sides of each wooden block. The lines should be spaced approximately $\frac{1}{8}$in apart.

Step 5...

Next take a pair of standard inexpensive tweezers and pull the two blades apart so that they no longer touch. Widen the tweezer's ends so that they stay approximately $\frac{3}{8}$in apart. Press the ends gently into the clay to form the vertical ends of the bricks. See picture 5. Repeat stages 2, 3, 4 and 5 with the remaining 2 balsa blocks. Leave overnight to dry out completely and harden.

Step 6...

Take a small ball of clay and a length of balsa wood approximately $\frac{3}{4}$in wide and $\frac{1}{2}$in deep. Roll out the clay into an even circle. Lay the flattened clay over the end of the balsa wood and press down so that the clay moulds to the shape of the end of the piece of wood.

.7.

Step 7...

Using a sharp knife, cut cleanly around the clay on all four sides approximately $\frac{3}{8}$in from the end of the balsa wood. Slide the excess clay off of the other end of the wood, leaving the sink shape in place on one end.

.6.

Step 8...

Take a cotton bud and cut one end off using a craft knife. Push the end of the cotton bud into the base of the clay sink to form the plug hole. Do not remove the sink from the end of the balsa wood. Leave to dry thoroughly, ideally overnight.

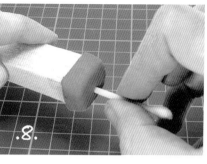

Step 9...

Once the sink is dry sand the edges smooth using fine sand paper. Paint the sink with 2 coats of 'off white' paint. I have used an eggshell finish for the sink depicted in this project.

Step 10...

When the paint is dry distress the sink with a little brown acrylic paint using the dry brush technique.

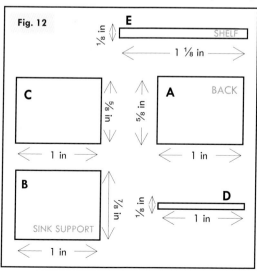

Step 11...

Draw out the shapes shown in *fig. 12 and fig. 13* onto mount board, then cut out each shape using a craft knife and metal ruler. Using a scribe tool or the blunt edge of a small pair of scissors, carefully score **part F** as shown in *fig. 13*.

Fig. 12

E — SHELF — $\frac{1}{8}$ in — 1 $\frac{1}{8}$ in

C — 1 in — $\frac{5}{8}$ in

A — BACK — $\frac{5}{8}$ in — 1 in

B — SINK SUPPORT — $\frac{7}{8}$ in — 1 in

D — $\frac{1}{8}$ in — 1 in

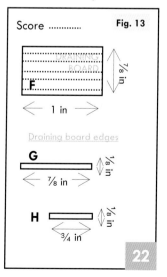

Score .... **Fig. 13**

DRAINING BOARD — **F** — $\frac{7}{8}$ in — 1 in

Draining board edges

G — $\frac{7}{8}$ in — $\frac{1}{8}$ in

H — $\frac{3}{4}$ in — $\frac{1}{8}$ in

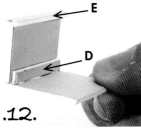

Step 12...

Using tacky glue stick **part A** onto the back of **part B** at right angles and allow to dry.

Next glue **parts D** and **E** into place, see picture 12. Glue part C in the position shown in picture 13. Clean off excess glue with a cotton bud.

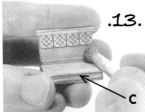

Step 13...

Paint with 2 coats of 'pale biscuit' coloured acrylic paint. Carefully cut out the set of 4 blue and white tiles found on page 46 and glue them to the back of the sink support. Using the dry brush technique distress with a small amount of brown acrylic paint. Set aside to dry.

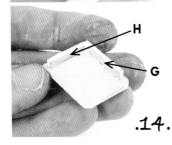

Step 14...

Glue parts G and H onto the draining board, in the positions shown in picture 14. Once dry, paint with 2 coats of brown acrylic paint, then distress with a little black acrylic paint. Set aside to dry.

Step 15...

Sand flat the ends of the 3 brick plinths, ensuring that the 2 smaller ones are equal in height. Sand the top end of the longest plinth at a slight angle so that when the sink unit is finally constructed, the draining board will gently slope towards the sink.

Step 16...

Paint all 4 sides of the brick plinths with the mortar paint mix, see picture 6. Work the paint well into the groves   between the bricks. Leave to dry.

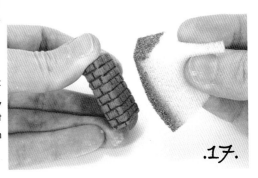

Steps 17 and 18...

Using a firm sponge and a little brick coloured emulsion, sponge paint the brick plinths gently ensuring that the paint does not go between the bricks. Paint all 3 plinths in this way and allow to dry. Next mix a small amount of black acrylic paint into the original brick colour emulsion in order to darken it and repeat the sponge painting process. When dry, glue the 2 smallest brick plinths to the bottom of the sink support, see picture 18.

.18.

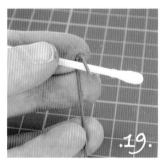

.19.

Steps 19, 20 and 21...

Take a small length of garden wire and bend the end section over a cotton bud to create an even curve at one end, see picture 19.

Next, using tacky glue, glue a small bead to the curved end of the wire and allow to dry. Paint with two coats of black acrylic paint.

When dry trim the wire to fit the sink and glue onto the back of the sink, see picture 21.

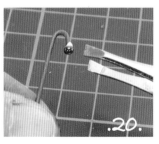

.20.

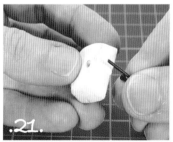

.21.

Step 22...

Finally, using tacky glue, glue the sink with tap attached to the top of the sink support.

Next glue the draining board onto the gently sloping end of the largest brick plinth, then glue the other end of the draining board onto the edge of the sink.

Leave to dry thoroughly before attempting to move the sink unit.

.22.

"Furniture..."

the dresser...

Materials...

- Mount card
- Medium card
- Tester pot of cream emulsion, cream acrylic or cream eggshell paint
- Brown acrylic paint
- x6 tiny beads *(for handles)*
- x4 5mm beads *(for dresser's feet)*

Step 1...

Draw out the shapes shown below in *fig.14* onto mount board.

Label each piece in pencil with the corresponding letter (as shown below), to avoid mistakes during construction.

Carefully cut out each shape using a craft knife and metal ruler.

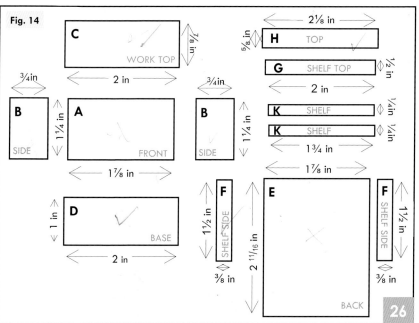

Fig. 14

C — WORK TOP — ⅞ in — 2 in

B — SIDE — ¾ in
A — FRONT — 1¼ in — 1⅞ in
B — SIDE — ¾ in — 1¼ in

D — BASE — 1 in — 2 in

H — TOP — 2⅛ in — ⅝ in
G — SHELF TOP — ½ in — 2 in
K — SHELF — ¼ in
K — SHELF — ¼ in — 1¾ in

F — SHELF SIDE — 1½ in — ⅜ in
E — BACK — 2 11/16 in — 1⅞ in
F — SHELF SIDE — 1½ in — ⅜ in

26

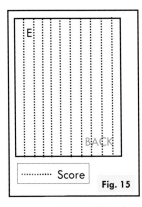

E

BACK

········ Score

Fig. 15

Step 2...

(This step is optional, complete it only if you require the rear of the interior shelf to appear as if it is made of planks) Using a scribe tool or the blunt edge of a small pair of scissors, score **part E** as shown in *fig. 15*.

Step 3...

Using tacky glue, glue the long edges of the 2 sides; **parts B** onto the front to dresser; **part A**, see picture 3. Clean away excess glue with a cotton bud throughout the construction stages.

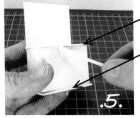

Step 4...

Next glue **part E** to the 2 sides; **parts B** to form the back of the dresser. See *fig. 16* and picture 4. Allow to dry.

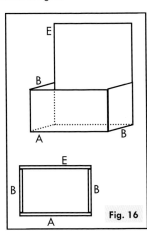

Step 5...

Glue on the dresser work top: **part C** and also the dresser base; **part D**. into place, see picture 5.

Fig. 16

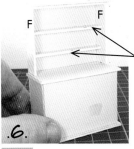

Step 6...

Next lay the dresser onto it's back. Glue the sides: **part F** x2 into place, positioning them on the inside edge of the back **part E** and touching onto the worktop of the dresser. Whilst the glue is still wet glue the back edge and ends of the two shelves; **part K** x2. and position into place. Remove the excess glue and allow to dry.

With the dresser still lying down glue on the shelf top; **part G**, ensuring that the back of the shelf is flush with the back of the dresser. When dry, glue on the top of the dresser; **part H** allowing it to over hang evenly all the way around, see picture 6.

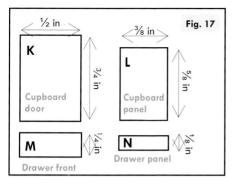

Fig. 17

K — Cupboard door — ½ in wide, ¾ in tall

L — Cupboard panel — ⅜ in wide, ⅝ in tall

M — Drawer front — ¼ in tall

N — Drawer panel — ⅛ in tall

Step 7...

Draw 3 of each of the cupboard doors and drawer shapes onto medium card and cut out. Glue panel pieces onto each door and drawer front. Glue drawer and door fronts into position on the dresser front, see picture 7. The measurements of both the cupboard and drawer fronts can be altered to change the finished appearance of the dresser.

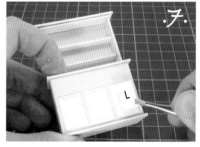

.7.

Step 8...

Paint the dresser with 2 coats of your chosen paint colour and leave to dry. Using a dry brush and a tiny amount of brown acrylic paint distress all over.

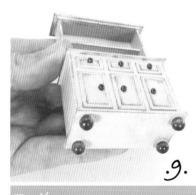

Step 9...

Glue x4 5mm diameter beads onto the 4 corners of base. Allow to dry.

Next glue x6 tiny beads onto both the drawer and door fronts, to form handles.

.9.

Top tip...

Pins can be used as handles instead of beads, simply push the sharp end into the dresser... or for an alternative look, try using different shape beads to give the appearance of a variety of handle styles...

For alternative colour combinations, try painting the work top, top and base a different colour to the main dresser carcass. Or paint with a dark colour and distress with off white emulsion for a worn, limed wood effect, see the interior pantry shelves on page 19...

a farmhouse table...

Materials...

- Mount card
- x4 matchsticks
- Off cuts of medium card
- Acrylic paint or tester pot of emulsion in cream.
- Acrylic paint or tester pot of emulsion in pale biscuit.
- Brown acrylic paint
- x2 small beads
- Tacky glue

Top tip...
The dimensions of this table can be altered to suit any project..

Step 1...

Draw out table top, see fig. 18, onto mount board and cut out with a craft knife and metal ruler. Using a scribe tool or the blunt edge of a small pair of scissors, score the table top as shown in fig. 19.

Fig. 18

TABLE TOP

A

1 ½ in

2 ¼ in

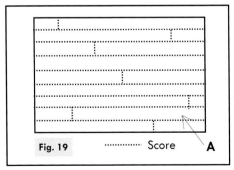

Fig. 19 .... Score **A**

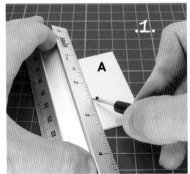

.1.

A

Step 2...

Mark and cut out mount card strips, as shown in fig. 20 on page 30. Glue strips: **parts C** to the end of **parts B** to create a frame shape. Leave to dry. Glue the frame into position on the underside of the table, see fig. 21 on page 30. Remove excess glue, see picture 2.

Step 3...

Next take the 4 matches and trim each one to a length of 1¼ inches.

Working with the table upside down position and glue the matchstick legs into the internal corners of the frame, see *fig. 21*. Ensure that the legs are completely straight. Leave to dry.

Step 4...

Cut 3 strips of medium card and cut to fit the underside of table top, see *fig. 21*. Glue into position. Cut 2 small strips of medium card and stick to the exterior of the frame to create 2 false draw fronts, see picture 5 below.

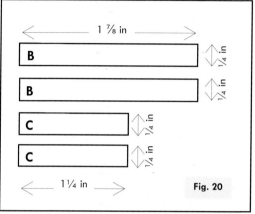

B ← 1⅞ in → ↕ ¼ in

B ↕ ¼ in

C ↕ ¼ in

C ↕ ¼ in

← 1¼ in →

Fig. 20

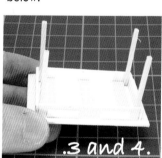

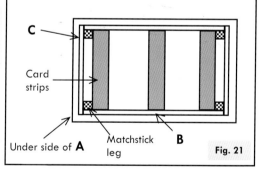

C →

Card strips →

Under side of **A**   Matchstick leg   **B**

Fig. 21

Step 5...

First paint the underside of the table with 2 coats of cream paint.

When dry paint the table top and it's edges with 2 coats of pale biscuit paint. Distress with brown acrylic paint using the dry brush technique.

Take 2 beads and glue them onto the drawer fronts using tacky glue, see picture 5.

.5.

30

a simple chair...

Materials...

- Mount card (off cut)
- 3 - 4 matchsticks (dependent on length)
- x2 regular paper clips
- Brown acrylic paint.
- Black poster paint
- Tacky glue & sand paper

Step 1...

Mark out **part A** shown below in *fig. 22* onto mount board and cut out carefully using a craft knife and metal ruler. Round off the front 2 corners of the seat base using the same method as the range cookers doors. See pg. 13, Step 5.

Step 2...

Onto the 2 rear corners of the seat base mark around a matchstick, as shown below in picture 2. Cut out the marked areas with a craft knife.

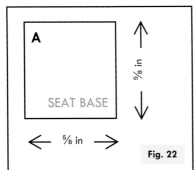

A

SEAT BASE

$\frac{5}{8}$ in

$\frac{5}{8}$ in

Fig. 22

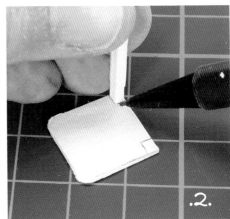

.2.

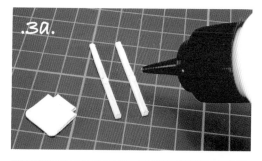

.3a.

Step 3...

Cut 2 matchsticks to a length of 1½ inches. From the base of both matchsticks measure up and mark the height of ¾ inch.

Below these pencil marks put 2 small blobs of glue, see picture 3a.

Position the seat base, **part A** at a right angle to the matchsticks, with the matchsticks sitting neatly into the small cut outs at the rear of the seat base, see picture 3b. Allow to dry.

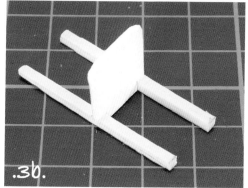

.3b.

Step 4...

Turn the chair upside down, for ease of access to the underside. Take another matchstick and cut 2 lengths: ⅝ inch long. Glue to the underside of the chair at right angles to the seat base, to form the front legs, see picture 4. Allow to dry.

Step 5...

Straighten out a paperclip. With wire cutters, cut small lengths, long enough to fit between the 2 back vertical supports of the chair. With the chair laid on it's back, glue them into place, see picture 5. Cut 4 more lengths to fit as cross members between the legs of the chair. Allow to dry completely.

Step 6...

Paint the chair with 2 coats of brown acrylic paint. Once dry, distress using the dry brush technique with a little black poster paint.

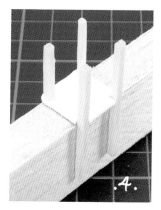

.4.

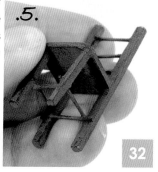

.5.

a butcher's block...

Materials...

- Balsa wood
- Mount card
- Acrylic paint or tester pot of emulsion in a pale biscuit colour
- Brown acrylic paint
- Red acrylic paint
- Small bead
- Paper clip (regular size)
- Medium card off cut
- 6 matchsticks
- Thin strip of black paper
- Tacky glue

Step 1...

Cut a piece of balsa wood to the dimensions given in *fig. 23*. Gently sand the edges and ends. With a scribe or sharp pencil, gently score along the dotted lines as shown in *fig. 24*. Then using a craft, knife shave off a little of the balsa wood on the front edge of the block, as shown by the shaded area in *fig. 24*. Paint the block with a little of the 'beam' paint mix, see pg. 6. Allow to dry before distressing, using the dry brush technique and a tiny amount of brown acrylic. For added realism, finally dry brush the front section of the block with a little red acrylic paint. Cut a thin strip of black paper and divide it into 4 strips about ½ inch long and glue onto the 4 corners of the block.

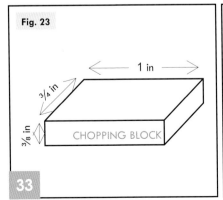

Fig. 23

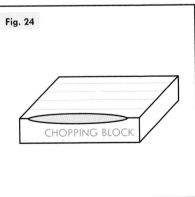

Fig. 24

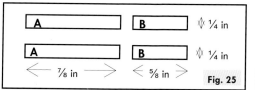

Fig. 25

¼ in

¼ in

⅞ in

⅝ in

Step 2...

Cut strips of mount card, as shown in *fig. 25*.

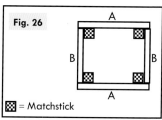

Fig. 26

⊞ = Matchstick

Step 3...

Glue parts A to the end of parts B to make a frame shape. See *fig. 26*. Allow to dry. Next cut 4 matchsticks to a length of 1 inch and glue into the internal corners of the frame as shown in *fig 26*. Allow to dry and harden completely.

Step 4...

Cut 2 matchsticks to fit between the legs and glue into place (see picture 4 below) to create 2 shelf supports. Next cut 2 slats from mount card: approximately ¼ inch in width and glue on top of the shelf supports, to create a shelf, see picture 7.

Step 5...

Take 2 pieces of hole punched card. Cut each circle in half and glue each half together to form two card semi circles. Glue onto the side of the butchers block frame, see pictures 5 and 7. Allow to dry. Glue a small rectangle of medium card onto the front of the frame to form a false draw front.

Step 6...
Paint the frame with 2 coats of chosen paint. Once dry, distress with a little brown acrylic paint, using the dry brush technique. Glue the butchers block onto the top of the frame.

Step 7...
Unwind a paperclip, measure and cut a length to fit snugly between the two semi circular card supports on the side of the frame, see picture 7. Glue the length of paperclip into place to form a rail. Take a small bead and glue it onto the false drawer front to form a handle.

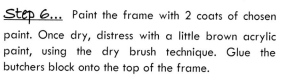

.7.

a plate rack...

Materials...

- Mount card
- Acrylic paint or tester pot of emulsion a pale biscuit colour
- Brown acrylic paint for distressing.

Step 1...

Onto mount board, draw out the shapes shown in *fig. 27*. Label each piece in pencil with the corresponding letter as shown below to avoid mistakes during construction. Cut out each shape using a craft knife and metal ruler. Using a scribe tool or the blunt edge of a small pair of scissors, score **part A**, as in *fig 27*.

Step 2...

Glue sides: **parts B** on the front of **part A**, then glue **parts C and D** to top and bottom, see picture 2. Leave to dry.

Fig. 27

E — FINIAL — 1½ in — ⅛ in

D — TOP — ⅜ in — 1⅝ in

A — BACK — B SIDE — B SIDE — 1 in — ¼ in — 1½ in — ¼

C — BOTTOM — 1½ in — 1⅝ in — ⅜ in

F — F — ⅛ in — ⅛ in

Score — SHELVES — 1⅜ in

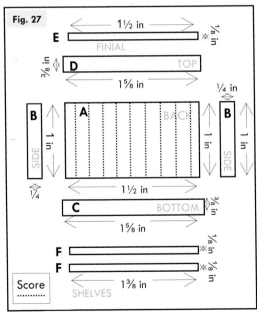

Step 3...

Glue the finial: **part E**, and shelves: **x2 part F** into place, see picture 3. Once dry paint with 2 coats of your chosen paint. Distress with a little brown acrylic paint, using the dry brush technique.

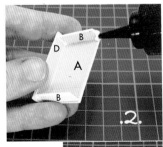

35

the coat rack...

Materials...

- Mount card*
- Medium card*
- x2 pins
- Medium brown acrylic paint
- Black poster paint
- Black permanent marker pen
- Tacky glue
- Wire cutters

only tiny off cuts required

Step 1...

Take an off cut of mount board measuring approximately ¼in x ½in. Next cut a slightly smaller rectangle of medium card and glue onto the front. Allow to dry.

Step 2...

Using a hammer and a pin, make 2 tiny holes into the front of the coat rack, see picture 2.

Step 3...

Paint the card with two coats of medium brown acrylic paint. Once dry, distress using the dry brush technique and a tiny amount of black poster paint.

Step 4...

Using a permanent black marker pen, colour in the tips of each pin. See picture 4.

Step 5...

Push the 2 pins into and through the 2 previously made holes in the card. Using wire cutters, trim the sharp ends of the pins that protrude from the back of the coat rack. Dab a tiny amount of tacky glue onto each pin on the back of the coat rack. Allow to dry.

"Kitchen room box..."

kitchen room box...

Materials...

- Foam core board*
  (¼in thick) or
  see 'Top tip' below...
- x2 - 6 pane plastic
  windows (see pg. 39 & 51)
- PVA adhesive
- Masking tape (optional)

*6mm thick wooden MDF board
can be used if desired, please
follow manufacturer safety
instructions when cutting &
sanding..

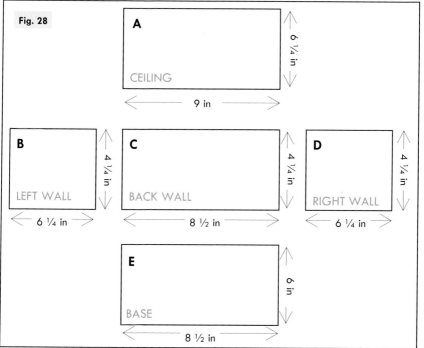

Fig. 28

A CEILING — 9 in × 6 ¼ in

B LEFT WALL — 6 ¼ in × 4 ¼ in

C BACK WALL — 8 ½ in × 4 ¼ in

D RIGHT WALL — 6 ¼ in × 4 ¼ in

E BASE — 8 ½ in × 6 in

(see pg. 39 & 51)

Top tip...

3mm thick card can be
used. Simply stick 2 sheets
together using a liberal
even coat of PVA adhesive.
Allow to dry completely,
ensuring that the card sheet
remains flat...

Step 1...

Mark out **parts A, B, C, D** and **E** shown above in
fig. 28 onto ¼in thick foam core board and cut
out carefully using a craft knife and metal ruler.
Please note: if you are using thinner card, the
measurements given above will have to be
adjusted accordingly.

Please note... For this room box, I used x2 plastic windows, with 6 panes (see page 51 for further details) painted in 'ivory' eggshell paint. The windows can be glazed with the clear lid of a butter pot etc. For the pantry window I simply cut down the window using a craft knife to make a smaller 4 pane window. The window positions given below are approximate and can be modified to suit your own personal layout or scheme. Using tacky glue, stick the windows onto the exterior of the room box.

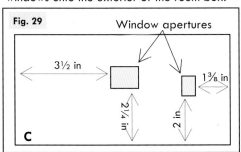

Fig. 29 — Window apertures

3½ in 1⅜ in 2¼ in 2 in C

Top tip...
Hold room box joins together with masking tape whilst they are drying...

Step 2...

Onto **part C** mark out window apertures as shown in *fig.29*, and cut out using a craft knife and metal ruler. Ensure that the window apertures are approximately ⅛ inch smaller than the window itself.

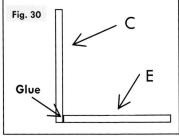

Fig. 30 C E Glue

Step 3...

At this point please follow instructions for the flagstone floor treatment to the base, see page 40. Once this stage is completed, continue to step 4...

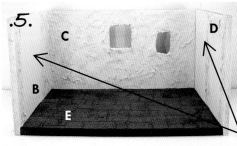

.5. C D B E

Step 4...

Using PVA adhesive, glue the back wall; **part C** at right angles to the back edge of the base; **part E**, see *fig. 30*. Allow to dry.

Step 5...

Glue on side walls; **parts B** and **D** onto each end. Allow to dry. Make pilot holes for hidden lighting: behind the fireplace and inside the pantry.

Step 6...

To complete the kitchen's rough rendered walls please see page 42. When the render wall finish is fully dried (and the pantry shelves have been dressed) glue the completed pantry, fireplace and cottage door into their final positions.

Glue the ceiling onto the top of the room box, fill and touch up the wall joins. Fit ceiling beam into place, please see page 43. Leave to dry.

flagstone floor...

Materials...

- Medium card, (with a textured surface is ideal, but not essential)
- 'Mortar Paint' mix - see pg. 6
- Grey poster paint
- Black poster paint
- PVA adhesive

Top tip...
Nail scissors are ideal for cutting out the rounded corners of the card flagstone shapes...

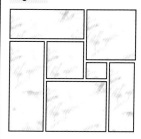

Fig. 31

Step 1...

Cut out random shapes of textured card, in a variety of sizes, see *fig. 31*.

Step 2...

Liberally spread PVA glue onto the base **part E.** Working on a small area at a time, stick down the card flagstone shapes, in a random arrangement. Ensure that all the edges of the flagstones are securely stuck down.

When the whole floor has been covered with card flagstone shapes, paint all over with one coat of PVA adhesive to seal the flagstones, particularly working the glue into the grooves. See picture 2. Leave to dry thoroughly and harden, ideally overnight.

.2.

Step 3...

Using the mortar paint mix, paint the whole of the floor, thoroughly working the paint into all of the gaps between the flagstones, see picture 3.
Allow to dry completely.

.3.

40

Step 4...

Put a little grey poster paint or grey emulsion into a saucer then take a small block of firm sponge and spread the paint mix evenly over the flat edge of the sponge. Sponge paint the kitchen flagstones using a light dabbing motion, ensuring that the grey paint **does not** go into the gaps between the flagstones.

Leave to dry.

Top tip...

You can mix your own grey flagstone paint by blending a tablespoon of white emulsion with a little black poster paint. To 'dirty' the grey paint, add a few drops brown paint to the final mixture, mix well...

Step 5...

Next add a few drops of black poster paint into the saucer and spread the darkened paint evenly over the sponge. Again lightly dab the paint onto the flagstones.

Once the floor has completely dried it can be sealed, if required by sponging on some quick drying matt varnish.

Different floor finishes can be achieved by cutting out alternative shapes from the textured card...

For example, try using even sized square flagstones. The appearance of the floor surface can also be altered by using alternative stone colour paints to represent different types of flooring materials...

rough rendered walls...

Materials...

- PVA adhesive
- Tissues
- Matt emulsion: tester pot in chosen room colour
- 'Mucky' paint mix: see pg. 6

Top tip...
To add a touch of 'dampness' to your cottage kitchen, sponge a tiny amount of moss green paint sparsely around the base of the walls...

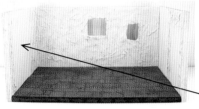

For a smoother plastered wall finish, simply substitute tissue paper instead of using matt tissues. Next, when applying the tissue paper, use small shredded pieces and do not allow the paper to crumple up. Finish by painting with a plaster colour emulsion, and then distress as before...

Step 1...

Draw round false doors or around anything that is to be attached to the wall, such as the panty shelf unit etc.

Do not apply render to these marked out areas, otherwise the doors etc will not adhere flush against the wall when they are glued in place once the render process has been finished.

Step 2...

Liberally coat the walls with PVA adhesive, then cover with shredded pieces of tissue sheets. Allow the tissue to wrinkle up and crease, as this will add texture to the final wall finish.

Allow to dry completely, ideally leave over night.

Step 3...

Paint the rough rendered walls with two coats of matt emulsion.

Leave to dry completely before distressing using some 'mucky paint' and the dry brush technique.

ceiling beam ...

Materials...

- Length of balsa wood
- 'Beam paint' mix -
  see pg. 6
- Black poster paint
- Tacky glue

Step 1...
Cut a length of balsa wood to the measurements provided in *fig. 32*.

Step 2...
Using a craft knife, cut away and round the edges of the beam. Add notches and cuts to age the wood's appearance, see picture 2

Fig. 32

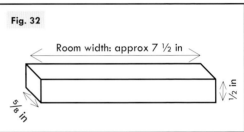

Room width: approx 7 ½ in

½ in

⅝ in

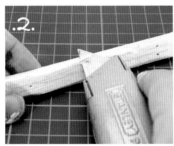

.2.

Step 3...
Apply 1 coat of the 'beam paint' mix, see page 6. Allow to dry completely.

.3.

Step 4...
Distress the ceiling beam with a tiny amount of

.4.

black poster paint, using the dry brush technique. Glue the beam onto the ceiling using tacky glue.

Top tip... For a limed wood finish, first stain beams to a desired natural wood colour, then distress with the dry brush technique, using a tiny amount of **WHITE** matt emulsion instead of a 'darker colour'...

cottage latch door...

Materials...

- Mount board
- Medium card
- Medium brown acrylic paint
- Black poster paint
- Small length of garden wire
- x2 pins.
- Black permanent marker pen
- Tacky glue
- Double sided sticky tape

False doors are both an easy and effective way to give the illusion of depth with in a room. They also help to give a property the illusion of depth, further rooms and also hidden areas...

Step 1...

Onto medium card, mark and cut out the main door shape, as shown in fig. 33.

Step 2...

Cut multiple lengths of medium card to represent the irregular planking strips on the front of the cottage door. Using tacky glue stick each length of card onto the door template, see picture 2. Next cut to fit and glue on 3 horizontal card 'planks' and 2 diagonal planks. See picture below

Leave to dry.

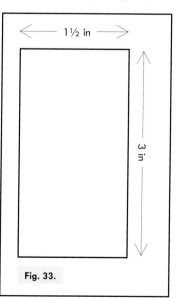

1½ in

3 in

Fig. 33.

Step 3...

Paint the door with 2 coats of medium brown acrylic paint. Leave to dry thoroughly.

Step 4...

Using a tiny amount of black poster paint, distress the door using the dry brush technique. See picture 4.

Step 5...

From mount card cut a strip approximately ¼ inch wide by 10 inches long. Mark 45° angles and cut the strip into 3 pieces as shown in picture 5, so that it fits snugly around the edges of the false door to create a simple door frame. Paint; repeat steps 3 and 4.

Step 6...

Place the door onto something soft (I used a spare piece of balsa wood) and gently hammer a dress maker's pin into the area of the door where your want the latch located. Repeat and make a second tiny pin hole next to the first.

Step 7...

Using a permanent black marker pen, colour in the two pin heads.

Step 8...

Push the 2 pins into the holes in the door. With wire cutters, trim away the excess protruding length of the pins from the back of the door. Fix the pinheads in place with a little dab of tacky glue onto the holes on the back of the door.

Step 9...

Cut a tiny length of garden wire and curve one end. Again using permanent black marker pen, colour in. When dry glue into place, laying the wire across the top of the 2 pin heads, see picture 9.

Step 10...

Fix the false door into position using double sided sticky tape. Next glue the door frame around the door with tacky glue.

tiles: to cut out...

Tiles for the pot sink...

Tiles for kitchen fireplace...

"Petite Properties..."

petite properties...

As a 1:24th scale dolls house builder I have made hundreds of different properties.
Each of my houses, cottages or shops are different and lovingly handcrafted as 'one off' creations.

My 'Country Town Collection' features an ever growing selection of period inspired properties and allows miniaturists to collect, display, fill and enjoy their very own personal and nostalgic street scenes.

"authentic architecture in miniature..."

Each Petite Property is specifically designed with a standardized depth, to allow each one to be displayed side by side to recreate traditional street scenes that celebrate the best in British architecture and heritage.

All Petite Properties feature an exclusive and realistic external finish, whilst the interiors are left as a blank canvas to allow their new owners to express their own creativity and imagination.

1:24th scale dolls houses available from £49.99

www.petite-properties.com

about the author...

Growing up I always harboured the urge to create. Throughout my childhood and teenage years, my Mum always nurtured my creativity and made sure that I was provided with a constant supply of cereal boxes, toilet rolls, yoghurt pots and most importantly, **inspiration!**

In fact, looking back at my childhood, I can't really remember a time when I didn't have my head stuck in a cardboard box, engrossed in gluing, cutting or painting and completely lost in my very own imaginary world.

One memorable Christmas morning I woke to find my stocking filled with lots of little knobbly parcels. On opening, they turned out to be little, simple pieces of wooden furniture. I was ecstatic and my mind immediately began to race with ideas for the type of wonderful 'box' house I could create to put them in.

Of course, downstairs waiting for me under the tree, was a wonderful 1970's style house complete with four open plan rooms and best of all: two real working lights.

To be truthful I can't remember anything else about that Christmas, just that I spent all of it moving furniture around and looking through the windows, finally understanding what it would be like to be a giant.

Unfortunately for my parents, it did not take me long to decide that my new dolls house needed some remodelling. Several cardboard modifications later and I had proudly transformed my house with extra partitions, secret doorways and not forgetting a new single storey 'shoe box' extension, which I had proudly and somewhat permanently glued on.

To this day, I whole heartedly believe it was at this very instance that the complete concept of **PETITE PROPERTIES** first sparked into life and the seed was sown deep inside my imagination. Now, some 25 years later... here I am!

Then...

...and now!

50

acknowledgements...

My love and thanks to...

Lucy, for her excellent editing and endless patience with me.
Mo, (Chloe) for her gentle encouragement, but sometimes brutal honesty.

And **Graham Tharby,** for his guidance and advice on all aspects of
'digital cameras and photography'.

Anthony Rivett [Tony] of **Pinchbeck Miniatures,**
for unwavering enthusiasm and support, right from the beginning...
when he helped me so very, very much.

I would also like to thank...

Jackson's Miniatures for their kind permission to use their window in this kitchen
project.
(_Please note_: Their complete range of 1:24th windows
are available to purchase from Petite Properties Ltd)

The Dolls' House Magazine, Guild Of Master Craftsman, Anthony Bailey -
for permission to use their front cover image of: **Issue 94.** featuring:
Fiona Broadwood of Petite Properties Ltd

Petite Properties Ltd.
www.petite-properties.com